S0-BIA-528

Nature Upclose

A Salamander's Life

Written and Illustrated by John Himmelman

Children's Press®
A Division of Grolier Publishing
New York London Hong Kong Sydney
Danbury, Connecticut

For Cindi and Bill Kobak, good friends who know how to enjoy a cold, rainy "sala-meander."

Library of Congress Cataloging-in-Publication Data

Himmelman, John
    A salamander's life / written and illustrated by John Himmelman
        p.   cm. — (Nature upclose)
    Summary; Illustrations and simple text follow a salamander through its life cycle, from larva in a pond through winter hibernation to spring mating.
    ISBN 0-516-20820-9
    1. Salamanders—Juvenile literature.   2. Salamanders—Life cycles—Juvenile literature. [1. Salamanders.] I. Title. II. Series: Himmelman, John.   Nature upclose.
    QL668.C2H56   1998
    597.8'9—dc21

                                            97-9128
                                               CIP
                                                AC

Visit Children's Press on the Internet at:
http://publishing.grolier.com

© 1998 by Children's Press®, Inc.
All rights reserved. Published simultaneously in Canada.
Printed in the United States of America.
            10 R 07 06 05 04

Spotted Salamander
Amybystoma maculatum

The spotted salamander is common in the eastern half of the United States. It lives in wooded areas and on hills that are close to freshwater pools or ponds. A salamander may live up to 20 years.

Look for spotted salamanders during the first warm, rainy night of spring. You may see hundreds, or even thousands, traveling from their burrows to the water. They lay their eggs in the water and then go back into the woods.

If you wrap a piece of red plastic around the head of a flashlight, you can watch salamanders without disturbing them. You may also see frogs and newts.

In spring, a salamander lays her eggs in a pond.

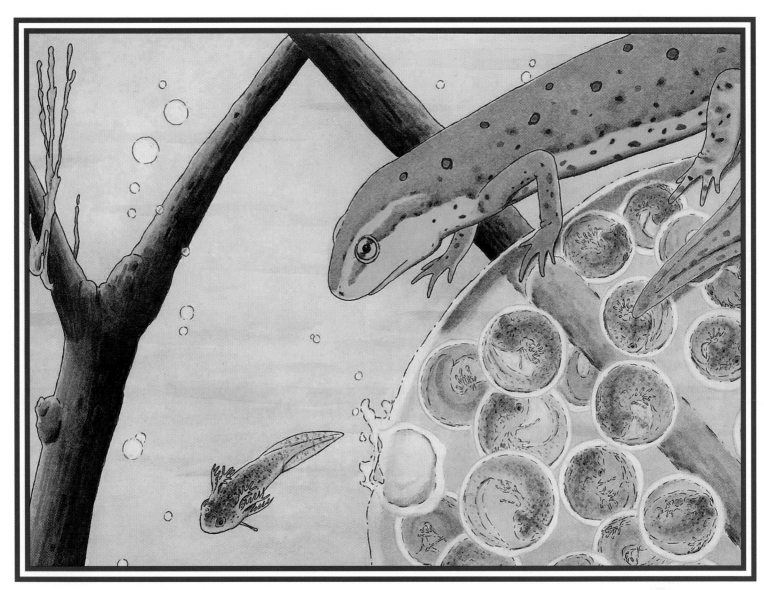

A red-spotted newt watches the first *larva* break free.

The salamander larva catches and eats a *copepod*.

A giant water bug would like to eat the salamander larva, but misses.

Soon, the salamander grows hind legs.

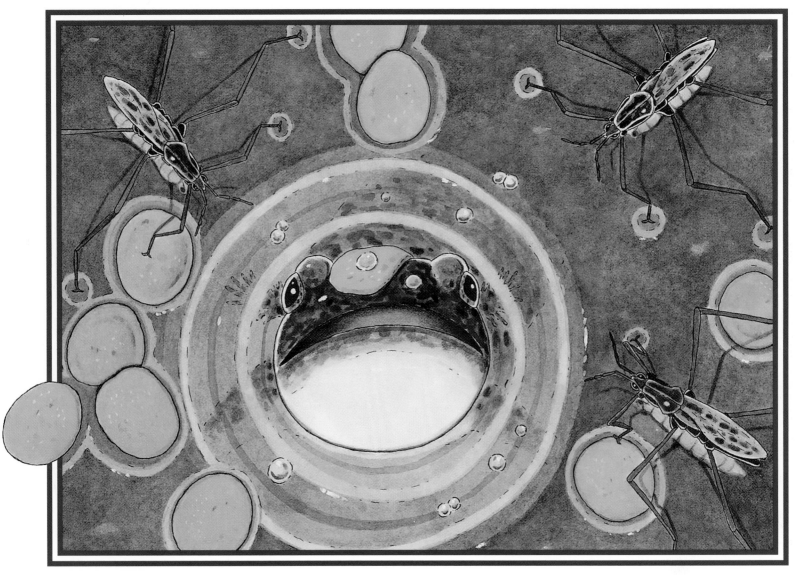

The salamander must swim to the surface for air.

At the end of summer, the young salamander leaves her pond.

She hunts for insects at the edge of the pond.

As the salamander grows, she moves farther into the woods.

A *milk snake* grabs the salamander . . .

. . . then lets go. Salamanders have bad-tasting skin.

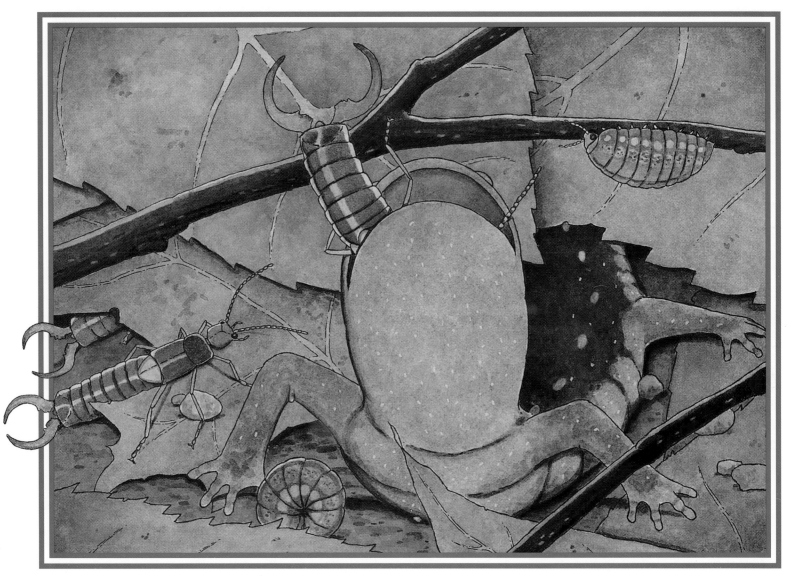

The salamander catches an *earwig* under the leaves.

As it grows cold, the salamander looks for a *burrow*.
A *deer mouse* watches.

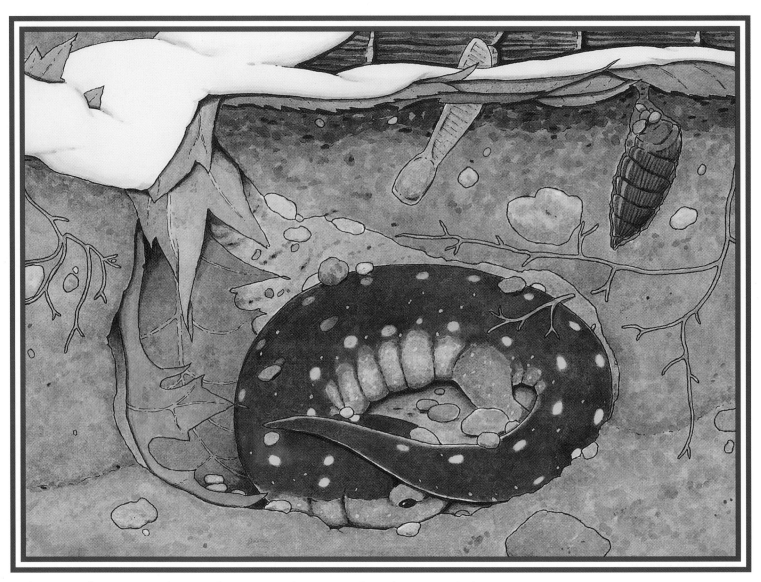

The salamander sleeps through the cold winter.

A rainy, spring evening wakes the salamander.

It wakes thousands of salamanders!

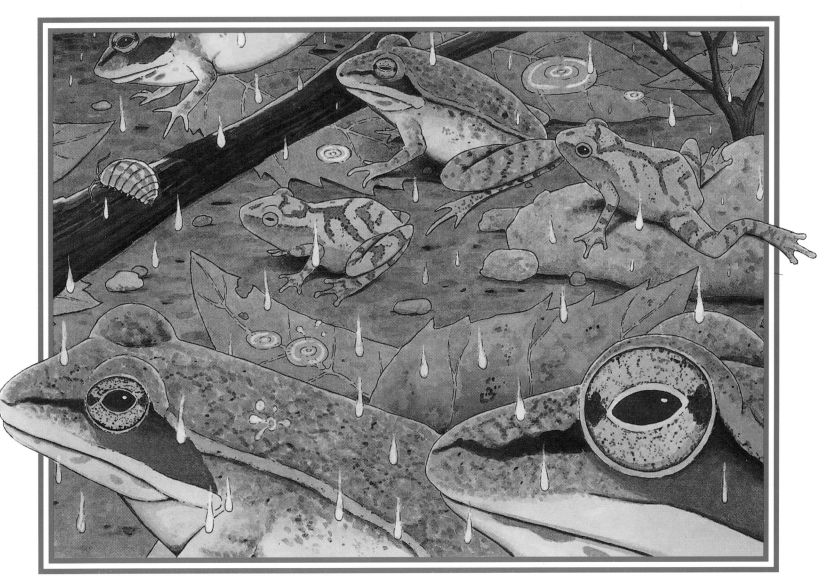

It wakes frogs, too!

A bright light falls on the salamander.

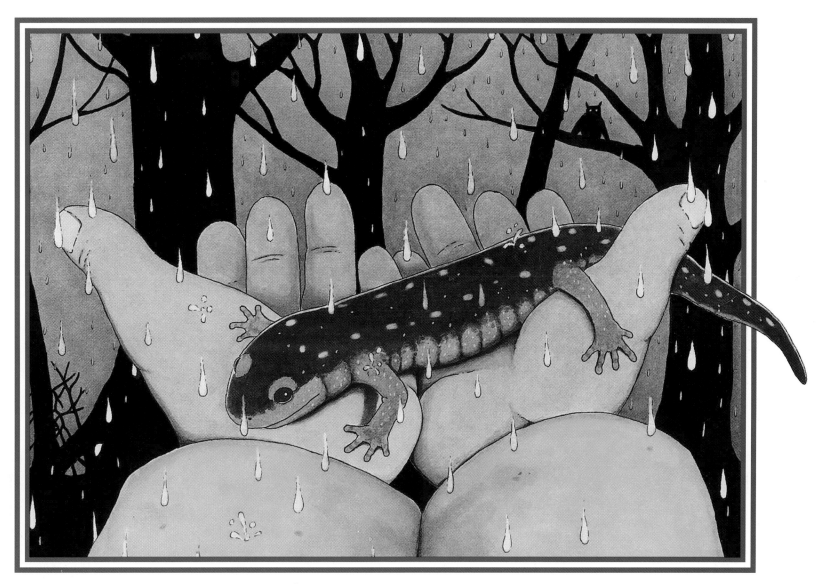

Gentle, curious hands lift her.

Then they put her back down.

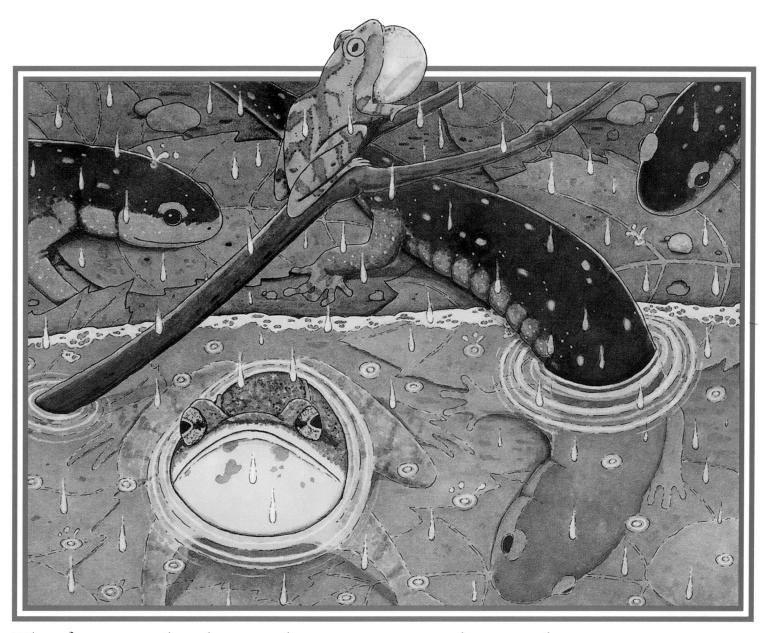

The frogs and salamanders return to the pond.

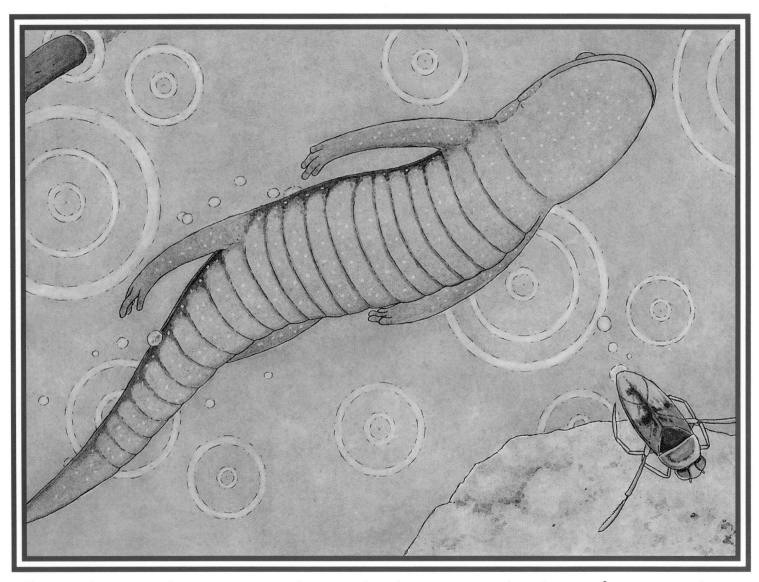

The salamander swims through the water looking for a male.

At last, she finds a mate.

Now the salamander lays eggs of her own.

She begins the journey back to the woods.

Summer night after summer night, the salamander hunts.

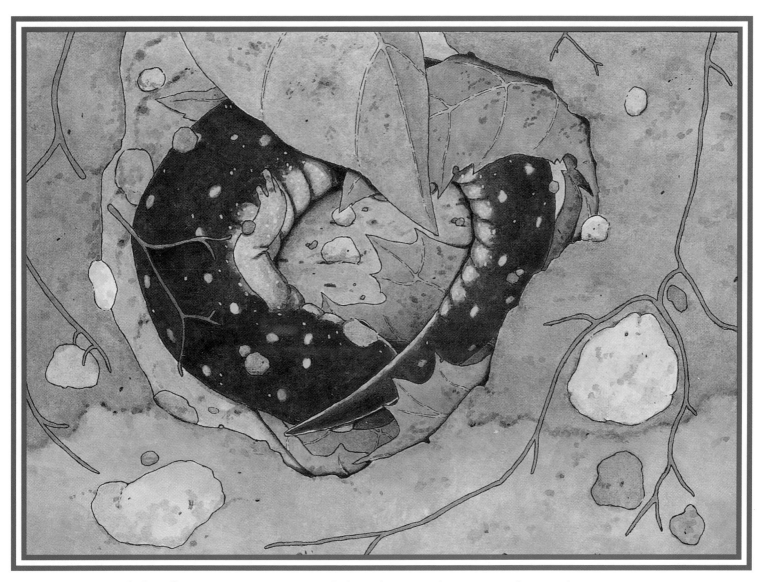

Winter cold after winter cold, the salamander sleeps.

And every first warm, rainy evening of spring, she wakes again.

Words You Know

burrow—a hole dug by an animal as a home.

copepod—a tiny animal found in many ponds, lakes, and the ocean. It is related to lobsters and crabs.

deer mouse—a small mouse common in fields and wooded areas.

earwig—an insect with sharp claws on its rear end.

larva—the first stage of a salamander's life.

milk snake—a brown and gray snake that eats insects and other small animals.

About the Author

John Himmelman has written or illustrated more than forty books for children, including *Ibis: A True Whale Story*, *Wanted: Perfect Parents*, and *J.J. Versus the Babysitter*. His books have received honors such as Pick of the List, Book of the Month, JLG Selection, and the ABC Award. He is also a naturalist who enjoys turning over dead logs, crawling through grass, kneeling over puddles, and gazing at the sky. His greatest joy is sharing these experiences with others. John lives in Killingworth, Connecticut, with his wife Betsy who is an art teacher. They have two children, Jeff and Liz.